Longman English Guides

PUNCTUATION

Ian Gordon

Longman

Titles in the series

Punctuation
Ian Gordan

ABC of Common Errors
S H Burton

Writing Letters
S H Burton

Titles in preparation

Spelling

Study Skills

LONGMAN GROUP LIMITED
Longman House
Burnt Mill, Harlow, Essex CM20 2JE, England
and Associated Companies throughout the World

© Longman Group Limited 1983

First published 1983
ISBN 0 582 20014 8

Set in 10/11pt Linotron Rockwell Light and Medium

Printed in Singapore
by Ban Wah Press

CONTENTS

page

Why punctuation matters   5

Capitals   7

    Special names   7
    Starting sentences   9

Full stops   11

    Ending sentences   11
    Making abbreviations   13

Questions marks   15

Exclamation marks   16

Commas   17

    Separating parts of a long sentence   17
    Separating parts of a list   18
    Separating explanations   20
    Separating words such as yes, no, thank you,
    does he, can't I   20
    Separating names of people spoken to   21

Apostrophes   24

    Possession   24
    Shortening words   25

Dashes   28

    Explanation   28
    Pauses   28

Direct speech   30

Quotation marks and underlining   34

   Quotations within quotations   35

Letters   36

Other punctuation marks   39

   Brackets   39
   Colons   39
   Semi-colons   40
   Hyphens   41

Revision   42

Answers   46

WHY PUNCTUATION MATTERS

When we speak, we do not say one word after another as though reading from a list. Instead, we pause between groups of words — sometimes for a very short time, and sometimes for rather longer. We also say some words with more force, so that more notice is taken of them. We move our voices up and down as well, and make "tunes" out of our speech. We change the expression on our face as we talk and maybe we move our hands. This too can make our meaning clearer. In all these ways we *shape* our speech.

When we write, we must also shape our words. First, we leave a space between the written words. When we speak, we run one word into another, but ifwedidthisinwritingweshouldfindreadingthough notimpossibleveryhardworkindeed.

Secondly, we use punctuation marks. Punctuation helps us to make our writing immediately and clearly understood.

This book explains the rules for punctuation as simply and clearly as possible.

Read it through carefully, and refer to it when you are not too sure of how to punctuate your writing. Do this regularly and you will soon punctuate well. You can then be quite certain that your readers will have no trouble in understanding and enjoying what you have written.

CAPITALS

Special names

Use a capital letter to start the names of *particular*:

people and titles

Tom	Dr Finlay
Jane	Queen Elizabeth
Shiva Ranjit	Sergeant Pepper
Miss Kate Brown	Inspector Wright
Mr Carter	Wai Lin
Mrs O'Sullivan	

places

England	Plymouth College
Moscow	Trafalgar Square
Europe	Mount Everest
the United Kingdom	Cyprus
the United States	India
the West Indies	the Atlantic
Fifth Avenue	the Red sea

days of the week, months, holidays, special days

Monday	Christmas
Tuesday	Boxing Day
January	Chinese New Year
February	Divali

languages, nations, religions

French	Africans
Spanish	Japanese
English	Christianity
Hebrew	Hinduism
Chinese	

7

books and films
   The Spy Who Came In from the Cold

NOTE Capitals for first and main words only

BUT no capitals for the seasons
   spring   autumn
   summer   winter

Use a capital for I
   Why was I born so beautiful?

Practice 1

   1 Write down the following names and titles using
     capitals.
     robert   president reagan
     chris   queen victoria
     miss lynne dart   inspector johnson
     mrs brown   superintendent walker
     mr true   captain bird
     dr who

   2 In each of the following groups *two* words only
     should start with a capital letter. Write them
     down. Do not write down the other words.
     (*a*) elizabeth   (*b*) paris
           girl   china
           boy   country
           thomas   place
           man   land

     (*c*) sea   (*d*) minute
           lake   september
           mountain   wednesday
           the pacific   month
           the himalayas   year

     (*e*) russian   language
           hinduism   church
           religion

3 Write down any of the following words which should be written with a capital letter.

chinese new year	new york
the black sea	green
table	mrs green
chair	school
river	college
the nile	

4 Write out these book titles and authors' names using capitals where necessary.
"cider with rosie" by laurie lee
"the hound of the baskervilles" by sir arthur conan doyle

5 Write the names of a friend, your doctor, a television personality, your town, today's day and date.

6 Write down the title of your favourite TV show and of a book you have read.

NOTE A missing capital can give the wrong meaning!
A fifteen-year-old Croydon boy has been suspended by his head since last September because of his long hair. (*News item*)

Starting sentences

Start each sentence with a capital letter.

All rooms have private bathrooms. Most face the sea. The hotel has its own swimming pool and restaurant.

Practice 2

1 Write the following five sentences with capitals at the beginning of each sentence.
who gave you that coat?
the holidays start in a week's time.
do you like music?
sword gang shoot up café.
don't do that!

2 There are *two or more* sentences in each of the following examples. Write the examples with capitals at the beginning of each sentence.

(a) do you have trouble in making up your mind? well, yes and no.

(b) the film will be ready next week. can you get it for me?

(c) my pen-friend lives in France. her name is Lucille. she writes very long letters. her English is very good.

(d) that's a big fish! where did you catch it? how much does it weigh? let's take a photograph of you with it.

FULL STOPS

Ending sentences

Put a full stop at the end of every statement sentence.

Before you meet your handsome prince, you have to kiss a lot of toads.
First prize was two tickets to Hong Kong. It was won by Mr Barlow of Winchester Prison. (*News item*)

Practice 3

Which of these groups of words are sentences? Write them down. Start each sentence with a capital letter. End each sentence with a full stop.

WARNING Do not write down the groups of words which are not sentences.

1 at seven o'clock
2 the concert starts at seven o'clock
3 after a long wait in the rain
4 we caught the bus after a long wait in the rain
5 birds fly
6 after the disco finished at eleven-thirty and everyone had gone home
7 i bet you i could stop gambling
8 coming to the top of the hill
9 instead of sending my friend a letter
10 in baiting a mousetrap, always leave room for the mouse (*Saki*)

Practice 4

Each of the following consists of one complete sentence. Write it with a capital at the beginning and for any other words that need capitals in the sentence. Write a full stop at the end.

1 i read an article about farming in wales last week
2 chinese children get red packets with money inside at chinese new year
3 queen elizabeth rules uk
4 in the philippines people can vote at the age of fifteen
5 the commonest surname in the world is chang

Practice 5

Write each of the following with full stops and capitals. The number of sentences in each example is given in brackets.

1 my camera is the latest i won it in a marmalade competition (2)
2 a woman was charged last week at hendon with stealing two pen and pencil sets she told magistrates that one was a present for her probation officer (2) (*News item*)
3 a young japanese boy wrote 700 letters to his girlfriend she is to marry the postman (2) (*News item*)
4 a seattle man who hi-jacked a plane demanded one million dollars in cash and a parachute after bargaining all day he changed his demand to three cheeseburgers (2) (*News item*)
5 an unknown man walked into a new york hospital and asked if he could give his body for medical research he was told he could the man then shot himself dead (3) (*News item*)
6 the town of thursby is very proud of its most famous son, sir thomas burch sir thomas burch

was born in thursby in 1822 and he died in 1880 his most famous construction was the forth bridge the bridge collapsed a year after it was opened and hundreds of people were killed (4)

7 the thief took out a large bunch of keys he soon found one to fit the door then he walked carefully down the corridor suddenly the alarm bell began to ring (4)

8 thank you for your letter it came this morning i was glad to hear your father is back from turkey you must be very glad to see him (4)

9 a boy took home a stolen cycle his father thrashed him and sent him to bed next day the boy wanted to put matters right by returning the cycle he found his father had gone to work on it (4) (*News item*)

10 collins parked his bike and hit the horse on the nose the horse backed away pushing its caravan into the car behind a man leading a goat across the road thought he could calm the animal he tied his goat to the railway barrier and held the horse just then the crossing keeper raised the barriers the goat was hanged (6) (*News item*)

Making abbreviations

A full stop is used to mark an abbreviation — the shortening of a word. It is also used after initials.

D.H. Lawrence	for David Herbert Lawrence
Market Sq.	for Market Square
S.W.	for south-west

The full stop is not generally used if the abbreviation ends with the same letter as the full word.

Barlow Rd
Mr and Mrs Smith
Dr Fenton

Practice 6

Write the following with full stops and capitals where needed.

mr j v strong   n e jones

new sq   dr f wright

manchester rd

QUESTION MARKS

Put a question mark at the end of every sentence that asks a question.

?

REMEMBER Do not write a full stop *and* a question mark together.

Have you an animal in the shape of a teapot? A cat maybe? (*Newspaper advertisement*)

WARNING Do not use a question mark in this type of *statement* sentence.

I asked him if anyone had an animal in the shape of a teapot.

Practice 7

Write these sentences with full stops or question marks at the end. Put capitals where needed.

1 can you please tell me where euston station is
2 i asked a policeman where euston station was
3 why don't you go to greece this summer
4 i read part of it all the way through
5 why not have the kids shot for easter (*Photographer's advertisement*)
6 i'm always asking myself why i'm always asking myself questions
7 have you change for a pound note
8 i couldn't understand any of his questions
9 have you any questions
10 is anyone really happy all the time

EXCLAMATION MARKS

Write an exclamation mark after a word or a group of words to show strong feeling — that someone is angry, or surprised, or frightened, or happy.

REMEMBER Do not write a full stop *and* an exclamation mark together.

John! Stop doing that!
Help! I can't swim!

Practice 8

Write capitals at the beginning and exclamation marks at the end of the following groups of words.

go away   there's Dave
get off   i've won
hold on

COMMAS

Commas separate parts of a sentence.

Commas help us to understand the sentence better.

Use commas *only* where you feel a pause is needed to help the sense.

Separating parts of a long sentence

When we got to the place where we had left the camera, we found that someone had taken it.
I never forget a face, but in your case I'll make an exception. (*Groucho Marx*)

Practice 9

Write the following sentences with
- a capital letter at the beginning of each sentence, and wherever else needed;
- a full stop at the end of each sentence;
- *one* comma where needed in each sentence.

1 after walking for two hours along a narrow path we found the bank of the river dove
2 if you can borrow a bicycle on sunday come along for a ride somewhere
3 there were plenty of gadgets for sale on the stall in the market but we could find nothing at all we were tempted to buy
4 you can make a dog lie down but you can't make him close his eyes (*African proverb*)
5 if you break your legs don't come running to me

6 all animals are equal but some animals are more equal than others (*George Orwell*)
7 do as I say not as I do
8 while there is life there is hope
9 money can't buy friends but you can get a better class of enemy (*Spike Milligan*)
10 cheer up the worst is yet to come (*Philander Johnson*)

Separating parts of a list

Unbreakable tea set: six plates, six saucers, five cups. £4. (*Newspaper advertisement*)

When cruising, stay on deck, eat only dry toast and tea, breathe deeply, keep your eyes off the waves, speak softly, and carry a big plastic bag. (*Travel guide*)

If 'and' is used before the last item, then the final comma is not generally needed.

Madame Vassilet of Russia gave birth to 16 pairs of twins, 7 sets of triplets and 4 sets of quadruplets.

Practice 10

Write the following sentences with
• a capital letter at the beginning of each sentence, and wherever else needed;
• a full stop at the end of each sentence;
• commas where they are needed.

1 the shark's stomach contained a pair of shoes a human skull and a copy of the bible printed on polythene (*News item*)
2 the road was littered for a hundred yards with broken glass torn metal and smashed packing cases

3 an exciting story interesting characters and a faraway setting are the things i most look for in an adventure story

4 our tour will give us a week in venice three days in florence four days in rome and the rest of the time we'll be travelling there and back on the coach

5 charlotte dod won the wimbledon singles title five times the british golf championship an olympic silver medal for archery and represented england at hockey

6 a golf ball hit by mr robert wilson struck a tree went through the windscreen of a passing moped and lodged in the driver's mouth (*News item*)

7 the airliner took off rose a few hundred feet in the air then suddenly dived into the ground and burst into flames

8 the lion looked up saw the hunter began walking towards him and then changed his walk into a fast and menacing run

9 richard simpson was detained in bolton royal infirmary with a fractured pelvis broken arms a fractured skull and internal injuries his condition is said to be comfortable (2 sentences) (*News item*)

10 mr john white was arrested for sharing his caravan with a donkey three grizzly bears thirteen dogs three rabbits nine chickens three peacocks five pigs five doves six pigeons a monkey a woman and eight children (*News item*)

Separating explanations

Note that *two* commas are needed.

The doctor, I am sure, will help you if she can.
Our cat, who loves fish, will not eat any sort of cat meat.

Practice 11

Write the following sentences with
- a capital letter at the beginning of each sentence, and wherever else needed;
- a full stop at the end of each sentence;
- *two* commas in each sentence.

1 margaret i'm quite sure would love to come with us
2 my brother edward you will be glad to know is now doing very well in canada
3 fishing just sitting around all day waiting for a bite seems stupid to me
4 gardening which i hate takes up most of my sundays in summer
5 some philatelists as stamp collectors like to call themselves spend a small fortune on their hobby

Separating words such as yes, no, thank you, does he, can't I

We sometimes make questions like this:

Your brother likes football, <u>doesn't he</u>?

The underlined words are called a "question tag". A question tag makes a statement into a question. A few other question tags:
isn't it? aren't they? don't you?

Question tags are separated from the rest of the sentence by a comma.

Words and phrases like yes, no, and thank you are separated in the same way:

Yes, that's my umbrella.
No, I'm afraid I can't come on Saturday.
Thank you, I'd be glad to come.

Practice 12

Write the following sentences with
- a capital letter at the beginning of each sentence, and wherever else needed;
- a full stop or question mark at the end of each sentence;
- commas where needed in each sentence.

1 you will come to see us won't you
2 your sister does learn yoga doesn't she
3 yes that is a good song isn't it
4 no this is not 637821
5 yes i've had plenty to eat thank you

Separating names of people spoken to

Sometimes *two* commas are needed.

Excuse me, sir, is this your jacket?
Your honour, I shot that pheasant because it was looking ill. (*Poacher in court*)

Practice 13

Write the following sentences with
- a capital letter at the beginning, and wherever else needed;
- a full stop or question mark at the end of each sentence;
- commas where needed in each sentence. There *may* be more than one comma needed in some sentences.

1 trevor must you leave your rubbish on the floor
2 now sergeant can you tell me why the police have taken my car away
3 and now ladies and gentlemen for something completely different
4 i'm all right jack
5 home james and don't spare the horses

Practice 14

Revision of commas.
Write the following sentences with
- a capital letter at the beginning of each sentence, and wherever else needed;
- a full stop or question mark at the end of each sentence;
- commas where needed in each sentence.

1 the isolation the loneliness the silence were getting on his nerves
2 the river was a problem fast-flowing deep enough to drown in and almost thirty feet wide
3 too amazed to speak he lay motionless feeling against his back the very slight shock of the boat striking the bank at last
4 she told the police she was going to commit suicide but the smoke got too thick and she couldn't breathe so she ran out of the building (*News item*)
5 the accused who pleaded guilty asked passers-by to help him start the car by pushing it along the road but unfortunately for him one of these was the owner (*News item*)
6 i'm very sorry paul but i did warn you the car had brake trouble didn't i
7 finding the race just too hard-going for him jim who is over fifty dropped out about half way but he says that he intends to enter again next year

8 abandoned by its owners or so we suppose the pup must have been without proper food for a week before we found it
9 if you can give me a ring mid-week i can bring the wood tools paint and everything next weekend can't i
10 opening the jumble sale mrs sale wife of the minister tried to make a joke about her name but no one understood it or at any rate no one laughed

APOSTROPHES

Possession

Use an apostrophe to show that someone *owns* something.

If only *one* person owns something, use 's.

Mary's car is very old.

If more than one person owns something, add the apostrophe after the s.

The gymnasts' skill delighted the crowds.

If two or more named people own something, use 's after the last person only.

John and Katherine's new house is much nearer the town centre.

Some words in English have special plurals without an s.

men   women   mice

Add 's to such words.

The men's faces were very frightening.

Practice 15

Complete the following. The first one has been done for you.

1 the car belonging to Elizabeth
   Elizabeth's car
2 the moped that Mike owns
3 the defeat of our team
4 the house belonging to John Ainsley
5 when Richard has his birthday
6 the playground for children
7 the courage of the policewomen
8 the kindness of my aunt and uncle
9 the cages the tigers live in
10 a strike of railwaymen

Use apostrophes for names of shops and people's homes.

I queued for nearly an hour at the baker's for hot cross buns.
Let's go to Clive's.
Everyone had a good time at the Johnsons'.

Shortening words

An apostrophe shows that one or two letters have been missed out.

I can't come today.   for   I cannot come today.
I'll come tomorrow.   for   I will come tomorrow.

An apostrophe is used when writing the time.
five o'clock   seven o'clock

Practice 16

Add one apostrophe to each of the following.
The first one is done for you.

1 Diana shouldnt smoke so much.
Diana shouldn't smoke so much.

2 Youll be sorry.
3 Dont you like swimming?
4 Im cold.
5 Whos the new prime minister?
6 Were certain to win!
7 Doesnt your brother ever stop talking?
8 Terryll phone tomorrow.
9 I shant be going to the match after all.
10 Wouldnt you like an apple or something?

WARNING Do *not* use the apostrophe for

his   hers   ours   yours   theirs

REMEMBER

its   =   of it
The cat drank its milk.

it's   =   it is *or* it has
It's raining. It's been raining all afternoon.

Practice 17

Add apostrophes to the sentences which need them.

1 Its time to go now.
2 Were a happy lot.
3 Theres a barbecue at the Wilsons every summer.

4 My mothers friends sisters going to the United States on Friday.
5 I think Ive left my jacket at Charlenes.
6 Whose turn is it now?
7 Whos the tall girl in blue?
8 Our club draws its membership from all over the town.
9 I didnt know your sister had a new job.
10 Theres some really cheap steak at the butchers this week.

DASHES

Explanation

Use a dash to introduce a comment or an explanation.

Soccer player Daniel Allende has been transferred for a record fee — 550 beef steaks. (*News item*)

I like fruit — apples, bananas, pears, anything.

The dash "explains" what you mean by *fruit*. You would *not* use a dash if you did not write <u>fruit</u>, but simply wrote:
I like apples, bananas, and pears, anything.

If a sentence continues after the comment or explanation, two dashes are needed.

My grandfather — the one who died before I was born — sailed all over the world.

Pauses

A dash shows a break in speech.

Ogden drew his gun and screeched:
    "I'll take you, you — "

Practice 18

Add one dash or two to these sentences.

1 We had to wait three hours for a bus there was a crashed lorry blocking the road.
2 I do not take many photographs film is very expensive.
3 A man was charged yesterday with possessing an offensive weapon six rotten tomatoes.
4 Mr Bowler was fined £1 for having four children on a bike one on the handlebars, one on the crossbar, one on the saddle, one on his shoulders.
5 The exhibition of modern painting it was the largest ever held in the town was visited by nearly 20,000 people.

WARNING Do not use too many dashes in your writing. Do not use a dash when you should use a full stop or a comma.

DIRECT SPEECH

Direct speech is writing down what somebody said in the words they used.

Quotation marks enclose everything actually said. The first quotation mark goes at the beginning of the words spoken, and the second goes after the punctuation at the end of the words spoken.

"I think someone, or something, is moving about in the house," Tom whispered.
"This is spooky!" I exclaimed.
"Should we go and investigate?" Mike asked.
"Well," I replied quickly, "it's no use asking me to go. I lost my glasses. I'm blind without them."
Even more quickly Tom came in, "And I'm no good either — I sprained my ankle. I'm crippled!"
"In that case," Mike concluded, "as you are so frightened I'd better stay here and look after you!"

Practice 19

Add quotation marks:

1 We always watch TV in the evening, said Jim.
2 Have you any money for a telephone call? asked the strange visitor.
3 If I give you some money, will you get me some flowers from the market? asked Mrs Lovering.
4 The man in the shop said, We've sold all the cheap postcards, I'm afraid.
5 Jean says she's too busy to come out tonight, said Maria.

Always start the first word of speech with a capital letter, even if speech starts inside a sentence:

The girl said hysterically, "It's David. They've killed him."

If a sentence carries on after the speaker is named, do not use a capital letter:

"In that case," Robert said, "wouldn't it be better to go out?"

If a new sentence starts after the speaker has been named, use a capital letter:

"We caught the slow train," he explained. "We didn't get home until midnight."

Practice 20

Add capitals:

1 the doctor replied, "you should be up and walking in a week."
2 my dentist shook his head and said, "i'm afraid i'll have to take out both teeth."
3 "but this," said angela, "is murder!"
4 "we must get her away," i said. "do you know where she lives?"

If the words spoken are an ordinary sentence:
It isn't an adder, Mum.
change the full stop to a comma when you add quotation marks:
"It isn't an adder, Mum," Tim said scornfully.

If the person speaking comes before the words spoken, add a comma before the first quotation mark, but leave the rest of the punctuation the same:
Tim said scornfully, "It isn't an adder, Mum."

If the words spoken have a question mark or exclamation mark:
What happened to the dog?
keep the punctuation the same when you add quotation marks:
"What happened to the dog?" he asked.

Practice 21

Add commas, full stops, capital letters, question marks and exclamation marks where needed:

1 "do you need a passport for a day trip" i asked
2 "what's on the television then" robert asked
3 "what a lovely surprise" i exclaimed
4 "thank you very much" i said "but i'll walk"
5 "some people" he complained "are never happy"
6 then she said "i hear there's a war coming on"

A speech may run on into two or more sentences. Do not add the last quotation marks until the end of the speech.

"This," I said, "has a very odd smell about it. Shall we cut across the fields and see what is going on?"

Practice 22

Add capitals and quotation marks. There is one speaker in each example.

1 we caught the last train, he explained, but it was very slow.
2 if you can't come, i said, give me a ring. i'll be home all evening.
3 after we'd paid for the boat, jonathan explained, we found it leaked badly. it'll cost a lot to put it right.
4 in the end, she said, we found the pet shop. it was close to the market.

Begin a new paragraph for each new speaker.

"I always thought space was dark and cold," he remarked vaguely.

"Forgotten the sun?" said Weston.

"If it's like this in the early morning —" Ransom began.

"Don't talk," Weston said. "The ship does not carry oxygen enough for any unnecessary exertion."

Practice 23

There are two speakers in each of these. Add capitals and punctuation marks. Begin a new paragraph for each new speaker.

1 "waiter" shouted the angry customer "what on earth is this fly doing in my soup" "i think sir" replied the waiter "its doing the breast stroke"

2 "i shall be back at seven o'clock" i shouted as i left the house "dont be late" brian answered "theres a good film on tv"

3 "thats harry over there" exclaimed susan "lets go and talk to him" i said

4 "are you fond of dancing" mark asked me "not very much" i replied shortly "why not" mark demanded "everyone likes dancing" "well i dont" i replied "i seem to have two left feet when i try to dance would you like to teach me"

5 "doctor im really worried i keep thinking im a pair of curtains" "pull yourself together" he replied

6 "gad bloodnok i admire your guts" "what are they showing" cried bloodnok (*Spike Milligan*)

QUOTATION MARKS AND UNDERLINING

Use quotation marks for an extract from a book, or for words actually spoken.

The witness said that someone called her husband "an old pig". She said that he was not old. (*News item*)

Use quotation marks for the titles of books, films, plays, magazines and newspapers.

Because of a shortage of money, the Open Air Theatre Company will now stage "Snow White and the Two Dwarfs". (*News item*)

Practice 24

Write the following sentences with quotation marks where needed.

1 Too tired is all Alan says if you ask him to wash up.
2 Cold, damp, expensive were the only words on the postcard.
3 A woman borrowed a book called How to Develop a Superpower Memory and forgot to return it.
4 Sell by 8th March was printed clearly on the label.
5 Henri IV of France called James I the wisest fool in Christendom.

Some people prefer to underline titles of books, films and plays, rather than using quotation marks, especially in typing.

She went to see <u>Love Story</u> seven times.

Underlining is also used to emphasise a word or group of words.

I was <u>so</u> tired and <u>very</u> angry.

Avoid using underlining too much for emphasising words. If you use it too much it will not be so effective.

Quotations within quotations

If you need to use one set of quotation marks within another set of quotation marks, use double for the "outer set" and single for the "inner set".

"Why didn't you say 'Hello' when you saw me yesterday?" Helen asked.
"I heard a splash and someone shout 'Help! I can't swim!' "I told the policeman.
"I've never read 'Alice in Wonderland'," Rachel admitted.

Practice 25

Write the following sentences with commas, question marks and quotation marks where needed.

1 Have you read David Copperfield I asked.
2 Have you a light the man asked and as I struck a match he hit me Ronald explained.
3 I heard a voice crying there's someone still in the house but I could not see anything for the smoke the witness told the judge.

LETTERS

Sample letter: notice the capital letters and punctuation marks.

> 15 Prospect View,
> Milldale,
> Sheffield.
> S2 8KL
>
> 1st May 1985
>
> Dear Miss Thomas,
>   I'm sorry that Mary has been away from school with her head. She's had it on and off all week.
>
>   Yours sincerely,
>   James Green

Sometimes it is useful to write the name and address of the person you are writing to on the letter itself as well as on the envelope. If you keep a copy of the letter, it will show clearly
- whom the letter was sent to.
- where the letter was sent.

You usually do this when you are writing a formal or business letter that you might need to refer to in the future.

> 2 Admiralty Street,
> Plymouth.
>
> 14th July 1982
>
> The Manager,
> "Young 'n' Smart",
> 15 the Esplanade,
> Bournemouth.
>
> Dear Sir,
>
> I bought the enclosed pair of jeans from your shop while on holiday last month. They are clearly marked "will not shrink." They are also clearly marked 32 inch waist. However, as you can see, after one wash, they are 28 inch waist. I should be glad of a refund, or replacement jeans, 32 inch waist, that you can be sure will not shrink.
>
> Yours sincerely,
> Clare Smith

An address included on the letter like this is called the *inside address*. The inside address is sometimes written at the bottom of the letter on the left-hand side.

Some people prefer not to slope the address. In typing, the address is not usually sloped and commas and full stops are often left out:

> 15 Prospect View
>
> Milldale
>
> Sheffield
>
> S2 8KL

Practice 26

1 Set out your own address as it should appear at the top of a letter.

2 Set out the following addresses as they should appear on an envelope.

   (a) miss alice ford 58 durnford street saltash cornwall pl12 4rd uk

   (b) mr thomas north 42 union street whitford-on-sea norfolk nr32 6rt

   (c) mr and mrs r c anderson the white house upton derbyshire s29 7dl

   (d) the manager universal book store 101 main street exeter devon ex2 3gq

   (e) the swiss laundry 2 george street chester cheshire ch1 1nq

3 Set out the following letters as neatly as you can on the page.

   (a) Use today's date. Use your own address.

   Dear Susan, Thank you for the box of chocolates. It was very good of you to send them. I am now out of hospital, and I'm feeling much better. I still can't write very well, as my wrist is swollen, so excuse this short note. Love, Paula

   (b) Haughty Towers, Nobleville, Proudshire. 5th June 1832

   My Dear Charles, Thank you for your kind invitation to a duel at 8 o'clock tomorrow morning. I am happy to accept. Unfortunately, I am a late riser. Though I shall try to be punctual, I must apologise in advance for any lateness. If you get tired of waiting, please go ahead and shoot. Your obedient servant, James Layabed

OTHER PUNCTUATION MARKS

Brackets

Brackets are useful for adding extra information.

The First World War (1914–1918) cost millions of lives.
Plymouth (population 249,000) is over twice as large as Exeter (93,900).
Women learn modern languages (but not ancient) more easily than men.
I have several original Mona Lisas, all painted (according to the signature) by the great artist Kodak. (*Spike Milligan*)
White has not always been the traditional colour for wedding dresses. (Mary Tudor wore black at her wedding.)

Colons

A colon can be used to introduce a list.

The garage found three things wrong with the car: faulty brakes, poor steering and a lot of rust underneath.
There were all sorts of boats on the lake: windsurfers, dinghies, speedboats and canoes.
We climbed four of the major peaks: Skidaw, Helvellyn, Great Gable and Pillar.
Glenda Jackson has won Oscars in two films: *Women in Love* and *A Touch of Class*.

A colon may introduce a comment or an explanation in the same way as a dash (see page 29).

I like work: it fascinates me. I can sit and look at it for hours.
The weather continued the same every day: hot all day with a storm at night.
The dogs began growling: they must have heard a noise.
You will recognize the first sign of age: it is when you go out and realise for the first time how young the policemen look.
There was a surprise waiting for us when we got home: the new car had been delivered.

Semi-colons

A semi-colon may separate the main parts of a long sentence.

Love is like the measles; we all have to go through it. (*Jerome K. Jerome*)
The cook was a good cook, as cooks go; and as cooks go she went. (*Saki*)
Every man wants to live long; but no man wants to be old. (*Jonathan Swift*)
To lose one parent, Mr Worthing, may be regarded as a misfortune; to lose both looks like carelessness. (*Oscar Wilde*)
Marriage is a very fine institution; no family should be without one. (*Anon*)

A semi-colon can be useful when a sentence has a lot of commas, so that the main divisions can be clearly seen.

We decided there could be three possible reasons why Mike had not arrived: he might, although this was extremely unlikely, have not received our letter; he might have received the letter, and his reply had not reached us; or possibly, and this of course was what worried us, he might have had an accident, got stuck in a snowdrift, or skidded off the icy roads.

Hyphens

Some words are always spelt with a hyphen:
For example

twenty-one   co-educational   self-important

If a word is too long to fit on the end of a line, it can be divided by a hyphen. If you have to divide a word in this way, remember to divide it by syllables. Write the hyphen at the *end* of the first line, not the beginning of the next line.

Michael is always find-
ing some bargain or other.

REVISION

Practice 27

Punctuate the following.

1 the high court ruled yesterday that a woman convicted of unlawfully killing her husband with a kitchen knife is not entitled to a widows allowance

2 my cousin louise speaks spanish and german very well but joseph isnt any good at languages at all

3 your friend lives in london doesnt he she said

4 tony can you get me practical gardening from the library when you go

5 i like hockey horse-riding and ski-ing in winter my brother hates any sort of sports but he likes making things

6 we found trevors pen-knife in the long grass its a very nice one with a pearl handle the blades are made of stainless steel which is lucky for him as it was lying outside all night

7 as i was reading a book my father got me for my birthday called ten best spy stories i fell asleep in my chair in front of the fire i then had a vivid dream in which i was james bond and i was a prisoner in a cellar a rat came and started to bite my feet i woke suddenly our persian cat was nibbling at my toes

8 during the visit he made to asia last summer with my aunt uncle keith took hundreds of photographs he showed some of them to us last night crowded indian streets and markets sampans in

bangkok rickshaws in hong kong temples in japan and so on he said that hes going to write an article called asia on the cheap for a travel magazine it should be a very good article

9 which is the quickest way to cawsand please if youve plenty of time to spare you can take the coast footpath she told me if you are in a hurry youd better take a bus the no 18 goes to cawsand how often are the buses i asked every half-hour theres one leaving in five minutes at 4 o clock the bus stop is just over there

10 when inspector john harding and sergeant ivan tower arrived they found him hanging by his fingertips from the window more than 45 metres above the ground they offered him cigarettes and coffee but he kept refusing

11 plans to break the world flame-throwing record at james brothers circus in waltham cross hit a snag on wednesday morning when 26-year-old karl alva sucked instead of blew in training

12 batsmen playing in southport second team against fleetwood in the northern league yester-day found runs frustratingly hard to come by then after more than two hours play the reason dawned on them fleetwood had 12 men on the field the mistake came to light when there were not enough meals to go round at the interval

13 my husbands mother was hawaiian and we thought it might be nice to give the child a traditional name said mrs seymour the mum of a 2½-week-old washington boy on why he was baptised keaminuimakahahaikalani

14 the jury had also heard from teena childs of her horror when she read in a newspaper report that her husband had murdered six people she said i thought he was just a normal bloke though he occasionally pulled out his toe-nails

15 sentencing the defendant the judge said you have a withered hand and an artificial leg and only one eye you have been caught in otley

leeds harrogate norwich beverley hull and york
how can you hope to succeed as a burglar

16 a game warden in india has put up signs banning
swimming in a crocodile-infested lake swimming
is prohibited survivors will be prosecuted say
the signs

17 returning to his car a motorist found it badly
damaged and there was a note tucked behind
his windscreen wiper it read i have just run into
your car people are watching me write this they
think i am giving you my name and address they
are wrong

18 a man in yugoslavia milivoja ristic has bought an
old bus which he plans to eat over a period of
two years mr ristic has already eaten 22,500
razor blades and 127 kilos of glass 3.6 kilos of
lead shot and a jeep ive always been like this he
said during the war i ate ordinary food and it
ruined my stomach

19 its really exciting ive never won anything like
this before a surprised mrs white said yesterday
afternoon my luck is changing the win provided
mrs white with the happiest moment since the
death of her husband four weeks ago

20 the inspector said that it was unlikely pollution
was the cause the fish bore no outward signs of
disease these fish are perfectly healthy except
that they are dead he said

21 two guests and two waiters were treated for
burns after a wedding cake exploded during a
reception at naples i think i must have used too
much alcohol in the mix the chef admitted

22 when he was arrested while driving a 25-year-
old mini roberts admitted he had no insurance i
broke my leg while trying to jack it up and i had
to get to the hospital he explained sergeant
adams said i heard the car from a mile away at
first i thought it was a bomb going off i approached the car which was going at about five
miles an hour and ordered the driver to stop i

found that it had four completely bald tyres neither hand brake nor foot brake would work the steering was poor there was no spare tyre and it would engage only in first gear mr roberts explained that he had bought the car for £5 his wife thought they might sell it to a car museum

23 a magician in zambia assured a small crowd that if anyone gave him one pound he would be buried alive for two and a half hours an onlooker gave him the money and helped to bury him after waiting for the time to pass the crowd dug him up the magician was dead his wife said something must have gone wrong a zambian pound is worth 53 new pence

24 an electrician from belgrade broke the world record for staying underground accompanied by a pair of canada ducks he remained below for 463 days during this period his wife divorced him

25 gardener alex wortleys home measures 1.4 metres by 0.9 metres by 1.4 metres alex who is 73 lives in a wood and metal box the box is in a back garden alex said yesterday everyone has a right to their own place and to me this is home i am happy here i have lived in boxes for more than thirty years i have had this one for twenty years

26 a piercing shriek cut through the silence of worthing magistrates court yesterday it was the sound of 36-year-old paul downs who was imitating the noise of a fork-lift truck mr downs was trying to demonstrate the type of noises that are keeping him awake at night

ANSWERS

Practice 1

1 Robert
  Chris
  Miss Lynne Dart
  Mrs Brown
  Mr True
  Dr Who

  President Reagan
  Queen Victoria
  Inspector Johnson
  Superintendent Walker
  Captain Bird

2 (a) Elizabeth
      Thomas

  (b) Paris
      China

  (c) the Pacific
      the Himalayas

  (d) September
      Wednesday

  (e) Russian
      Hinduism

3 Chinese New Year
  Black Sea
  Nile

  New York
  Mrs Green

4 "Cider with Rosie" by Laurie Lee
  "The Hound of the Baskervilles" by Sir Arthur
  Conan Doyle

Practice 2

1 Who gave you that coat?
  The holidays start in a week's time.
  Do you like music?
  Sword gang shoot up café.
  Don't do that!

2 (a) Do you have trouble in making up your mind?
      Well, yes and no.

(b) The film will be ready next week. Can you get it for me?

(c) My pen-friend lives in France. Her name is Lucille. She writes very long letters. Her English is very good.

(d) That's a big fish! Where did you catch it? How much does it weigh? Let's take a photograph of you with it.

Practice 3

2 The concert starts at seven o'clock.
4 We caught the bus after a long wait in the rain.
5 Birds fly.
7 I bet you I could stop gambling.
10 In baiting a mousetrap, always leave room for the mouse.

Practice 4

1 I read an article about farming in Wales last week.
2 Chinese children get red packets with money inside at Chinese New Year.
3 Queen Elizabeth rules UK.
4 In the Philippines people can vote at the age of fifteen.
5 The commonest surname in the world is Chang.

Practice 5

1 My camera is the latest. I won it in a marmalade competition.
2 A woman was charged last week at Hendon with stealing two pen and pencil sets. She told magistrates that one was a present for her probation officer.
3 A young Japanese boy wrote 700 letters to his girlfriend. She is to marry the postman.

4 A Seattle man who hi-jacked a plane demanded one million dollars in cash and a parachute. After bargaining all day he changed his demand to three cheeseburgers.

5 An unknown man walked into a New York hospital and asked if he could give his body for medical research. He was told he could. The man then shot himself dead.

6 The town of Thursby is very proud of its most famous son, Sir Thomas Burch. Sir Thomas Burch was born in Thursby in 1833 and he died in 1880. His most famous construction was the Forth Bridge. The bridge collapsed a year after it was opened and hundreds of people were killed.

7 The thief took out a large bunch of keys. He soon found one to fit the door. Then he walked carefully down the corridor. Suddenly the alarm bell began to ring.

8 Thank you for your letter. It came this morning. I was glad to hear your father is back from Turkey. You must be very glad to see him.

9 A boy took home a stolen cycle. His father thrashed him and sent him to bed. Next day the boy wanted to put matters right by returning the cycle. He found his father had gone to work on it.

10 Collins parked his bike and hit the horse on the nose. The horse backed away pushing its caravan into the car behind. A man leading a goat across the road thought he could calm the animal. He tied his goat to the railway barrier and held the horse. Just then the crossing keeper raised the barriers. The goat was hanged.

Practice 6

Mr J.V. Strong
New Sq.
Manchester Rd

N.E. Jones
Dr F. Wright

Practice 7

1 Can you please tell me where Euston Station is?
2 I asked a policeman where Euston Station was.
3 Why don't you go to Greece this summer?
4 I read part of it all the way through.
5 Why not have the kids shot for Easter?
6 I'm always asking myself why I'm always asking myself questions.
7 Have you change for a pound note?
8 I couldn't understand any of his questions.
9 Have you any questions?
10 Is anyone really happy all the time?

Practice 8

Go away!
Get off!
Hold on!

There's Dave!
I've won!

Practice 9

1 After walking for two hours along a narrow path, we found the bank of the River Dove.
2 If you can borrow a bicycle on Sunday, come along for a ride somewhere.
3 There were plenty of gadgets for sale on the stall in the market, but we could find nothing at all we were tempted to buy.
4 You can make a dog lie down, but you can't make him close his eyes.
5 If you break your legs, don't come running to me.

6 All animals are equal, but some animals are more equal than others.
7 Do as I say, not as I do.
8 While there is life, there is hope.
9 Money can't buy friends, but you can get a better class of enemy.
10 Cheer up, the worst is yet to come.

Practice 10

Note: Commas in brackets are optional.

1 The shark's stomach contained a pair of shoes, a human skull, and a copy of the Bible printed on polythene.
2 The road was littered for a hundred yards with broken glass, torn metal, and smashed packing cases.
3 An exciting story, interesting characters, and a faraway setting are the things I most look for in an adventure story.
4 Our tour will give us a week in Venice, three days in Florence, four days in Rome, and the rest of the time we'll be travelling there and back on the coach.
5 Charlotte Dod won the Wimbledon singles title five times, the British Golf Championship, an Olympic silver medal for archery(,) and represented England at hockey.
6 A golf ball hit by Mr Robert Wilson struck a tree, went through the windscreen of a passing moped(,) and lodged in the driver's mouth.
7 The airliner took off, rose a few hundred feet in the air, then suddenly dived into the ground(,) and burst into flames.
8 The lion looked up, saw the hunter, began walking towards him(,) and then changed his walk into a fast and menacing run.
9 Richard Simpson was detained in Bolton Royal Infirmary with a fractured pelvis, broken

arms, a fractured skull, and internal injuries. His condition is said to be comfortable.

10 Mr John White was arrested for sharing his caravan with a donkey, three grizzly bears, thirteen dogs, three rabbits, nine chickens, three peacocks, five pigs, five doves, six pigeons, a monkey, a woman, and eight children.

Practice 11

1 Margaret, I'm quite sure, would love to come with us.
2 My brother Edward, you will be glad to know, is now doing well in Canada.
3 Fishing, just sitting around all day waiting for a bite, seems stupid to me.
4 Gardening, which I hate, takes up most of my Sundays in summer.
5 Some philatelists, as stamp collectors like to call themselves, spend a small fortune on their hobby.

Practice 12

1 You will come to see us, won't you?
2 Your sister does learn yoga, doesn't she?
3 Yes, that is a good song, isn't it?
4 No, this is not 637821.
5 Yes, I've had plenty to eat, thank you.

Practice 13

1 Trevor, must you leave your rubbish on the floor?
2 Now, Sergeant, can you tell me why the police have taken my car away?
3 And now, ladies and gentlemen, for something completely different.
4 I'm all right, Jack.
5 Home, James, and don't spare the horses.

Practice 14

Note: Commas in brackets are optional.

1 The isolation, the loneliness, the silence were getting on his nerves.

2 The river was a problem, fast-flowing, deep enough to drown in(,) and almost thirty feet wide.

3 Too amazed to speak, he lay motionless, feeling against his back the very slight shock of the boat striking the bank at last.

4 She told the police she was going to commit suicide, but the smoke got too thick, and she couldn't breathe, so she ran out of the building.

5 The accused, who pleaded guilty, asked passers-by to help him start the car by pushing it along the road, but unfortunately for him one of these was the owner.

6 I'm very sorry, Paul, but I did warn you the car had brake trouble, didn't I?

7 Finding the race just too hard-going for him, Jim, who is over fifty, dropped out about half way, but he says that he intends to enter again next year.

8 Abandoned by its owners, or so we suppose, the pup must have been without proper food for a week before we found it.

9 If you can give me a ring mid-week I can bring the wood, tools, paint, and everything next weekend, can't I?

10 Opening the jumble sale, Mrs Sale, wife of the minister, tried to make a joke about her name, but no one understood it, or at any rate no one laughed.

Practice 15

2 Mike's moped
3 our team's defeat
4 John Ainsley's house
5 Richard's birthday
6 the children's playground
7 the policewomen's courage
8 my aunt and uncle's kindness
9 the tigers' cages
10 the railwaymen's strike

Practice 16

2 You'll be sorry
3 Don't you like swimming?
4 I'm cold.
5 Who's the new prime minister?
6 We're certain to win!
7 Doesn't your brother ever stop talking?
8 Terry'll phone tomorrow.
9 I shan't be going to the match after all.
10 Wouldn't you like an apple or something?

Practice 17

1 It's time to go now.
2 We're a happy lot.
3 There's a barbecue at the Wilsons' every summer.
4 My mother's friend's sister's going to the United States on Friday.
5 I think I've left my jacket at Charlene's.
6 Whose turn is it now?
7 Who's the tall girl in blue?
8 Our club draws its membership from all over the town.
9 I didn't know your sister had a new job.
10 There's some really cheap steak at the butcher's this week.

Practice 18

1 We had to wait three hours for a bus — there was a crashed lorry blocking the road.
2 I do not take many photographs — film is very expensive.
3 A man was charged yesterday with possessing an offensive weapon — six rotten tomatoes.
4 Mr Bowler was fined £1 for having four children on a bike — one on the handlebars, one on the crossbar, one on the saddle, one on his shoulders.
5 The exhibition of modern painting — it was the largest ever held in the town — was visited by nearly 20,000 people.

Practice 19

1 "We always watch TV in the evening," said Jim.
2 "Have you any money for a telephone call?" asked the strange visitor.
3 "If I give you some money, will you get me some flowers from the market?" asked Mrs Lovering.
4 The man in the shop said, "We've sold all the cheap postcards, I'm afraid."
5 "Jean says she's too busy to come out tonight," said Maria.

Practice 20

1 The doctor replied, "You should be up and walking in a week."
2 My dentist shook his head and said, "I'm afraid I'll have to take out both teeth."
3 "But this," said Angela, "is murder!"
4 "We must get her away," I said. "Do you know where she lives?"

Practice 21

1 "Do you need a passport for a day trip?" I asked.
2 "What's on the television, then?" Robert asked.
3 "What a lovely surprise!" I exclaimed.
4 "Thank you very much," I said, "but I'll walk."
5 "Some people," he complained, "are never happy."
6 Then she said, "I hear there's a war coming on."

Practice 22

1 "We caught the last train," he explained, "but it was very slow."
2 "If you can't come," I said, "give me a ring. I'll be home all evening."
3 "After we'd paid for the boat," Jonathan explained, "we found it leaked badly. It'll cost a lot to put it right."
4 "In the end," she said, "we found the pet shop. It was close to the market."

Practice 23

1   "Waiter," shouted the angry customer, "what on earth is this fly doing in my soup?"
   "I think, sir," replied the waiter, "it's doing the breast stroke."
   or "Waiter!" shouted the angry customer. "What on earth is this fly doing in my soup?"
2   "I shall be back at seven o'clock," I shouted as I left the house.
   "Don't be late," Brian answered. "There's a good film on TV."
3   "That's Harry over there!" exclaimed Susan.
   "Let's go and talk to him," I said.

4   "Are you fond of dancing?" Mark asked me.
"Not very much," I replied shortly.
"Why not?" Mark demanded. "Everyone likes dancing."
"Well(,) I don't," I replied. "I seem to have two left feet when I try to dance. Would you like to teach me?"
5   "Doctor, I'm really worried. I keep thinking I'm a pair of curtains."
"Pull yourself together!" he replied.
or "Doctor, I'm really worried – I keep thinking I'm a pair of curtains."
6   "Gad, Bloodnok, I admire your guts!"
"What! Are they showing?" cried Bloodnok.

Practice 24

Note: Punctuation in brackets is optional.

1 "Too tired(!)" is all Alan says if you ask him to wash up.
2 "Cold, damp, expensive" were the only words on the postcard.
3 A woman borrowed a book called "How to Develop a Superpower Memory" and forgot to return it.
4 "Sell by 8th March" was printed clearly on the label.
5 Henry IV of France called James I "the wisest fool in Christendom".

Practice 25

1 "Have you read 'David Copperfield'?" I asked.
2 " 'Have you a light?' the man asked, and as I struck a match, he hit me," Ronald explained.
3 "I heard a voice crying 'There's someone still in the house', but I could not see anything for the smoke," the witness told the judge.

2 (a) Miss Alice Ford   *or* Miss Alice Ford,
      58 Durnfold Street   58 Durnfold Street,
      Saltash   Saltash,
      Cornwall   Cornwall.
      PL12 4RD   PL12 4RD
      UK   UK

  (b) Mr Thomas North   *or* Mr Thomas North,
      42 Union Street   42 Union Street,
      Whitford-on-Sea   Whitford-on-Sea,
      Norfolk   Norfolk.
      NR32 6RT   NR32 6RT

  (c) Mr and Mrs R.C.   *or* Mr and Mrs R.C.
      Anderson   Anderson,
      The White House   The White House,
      Upton   Upton,
      Derbyshire   Derbyshire.
      S29 7DL   S29 7DL

  (d) The Manager   *or* The Manager,
      Universal Book   Universal Book
      Store   Store,
      101 Main Street   101 Main Street,
      Exeter   Exeter,
      Devon   Devon.
      EX2 3GQ   EX2 3GQ

  (e) The Swiss Laundry *or* The Swiss Laundry,
      2 George Street   2 George Street,
      Chester   Chester,
      Cheshire   Cheshire,
      CH1 1NQ   CH1 1NQ

Note: Some people also like to put a comma after the number of the house, e.g. 58, Durnfold Street.

3 (a)

Dear Susan,

Thank you for the box of chocolates. It was very good of you to send them. I am now out of hospital, and I'm feeling much better. I still can't write very well, as my wrist is swollen, so excuse this short note.

Love,

Paula

(b)

Haughty Towers,
Nobleville,
Proudshire.
5th June 1832

My Dear Charles,

Thank you for your kind invitation to a duel at 8 o'clock tomorrow morning. I am happy to accept. Unfortunately, I am a late riser. Though I shall try to be punctual, I must apologise in advance for any lateness. If you get tired of waiting, please go ahead and shoot.

Your obedient servant,

James Layabed

Practice 27

Note: Commas in brackets are optional.

1 The High Court ruled yesterday that a woman convicted of unlawfully killing her husband with a kitchen knife is not entitled to a widow's allowance.

2 My cousin Louise speaks Spanish and German very well, but Joseph isn't any good at languages at all.

3 "Your friend lives in London, doesn't he?" she said.

4 Tony, can you get me "Practical Gardening" from the library when you go?

5 I like hockey, horse-riding, and ski-ing in winter. My brother hates any sort of sports, but he likes making things.

6 We found Trevor's pen-knife in the long grass. It's a very nice one with a pearl handle. The blades are made of stainless steel, which is lucky for him(,) as it was lying outside all night.

7 As I was reading a book my father got me for my birthday called "Ten Best Spy Stories", I fell asleep in my chair in front of the fire. I then had a vivid dream in which I was James Bond and I was a prisoner in a cellar. A rat came and started to bite my feet. I woke up suddenly. Our Persian cat was nibbling at my toes.

   or I woke up suddenly — our Persian cat was nibbling at my toes.

8 During the visit he made to Asia last summer with my aunt, Uncle Keith took hundreds of photographs. He showed some of them to us last night — crowded Indian streets and markets, sampans in Bangkok, rickshaws in Hong Kong, temples in Japan, and so on. He said that he's going to write an article called "Asia on the Cheap" for a travel magazine. It should be a very good article.

9   "Which is the quickest way to Cawsand, please?"

"If you have plenty of time to spare, you can take the coast footpath," she told me. "If you are in a hurry, you'd better take a bus. The no. 18 goes to Cawsand."

"How often are the buses?" I asked.

"Every half-hour. There's one leaving in five minutes, at 4 o'clock. The bus-stop is just over there."

10   When Inspector John Harding and Sergeant Ivan Tower arrived(,) they found him hanging by his fingertips from the window more than 45 metres above the ground. They offered him cigarettes and coffee(,) but he kept refusing.

11   Plans to break the world flame-throwing record at James Brothers' Circus in Waltham Cross hit a snag on Wednesday morning(,) when 26-year-old Karl Alva sucked instead of blew in training.

12   Batsmen playing in Southport second team against Fleetwood in the Northern League yesterday found runs frustratingly hard to come by. Then(,) after more than two hours' play(,) the reason dawned on them – Fleetwood had 12 men on the field. The mistake came to light when there were not enough meals to go round at the interval.

13   "My husband's mother was Hawaiian, and we thought it might be nice to give the child a traditional name," said Mrs Seymour, the mum of a 2½-week-old Washington boy, on why he was baptised Keaminuimakahahaikalani.

14   The jury had also heard from Teena Childs of her horror when she read in a newspaper report that her husband had murdered six people. She said, "I thought he was just a normal bloke, though he occasionally pulled out his toenails."

15   Sentencing the defendant, the judge said, "You have a withered hand, an artificial leg, and only one eye. You have been caught in Otley, Leeds,

Harrogate, Norwich, Beverley, Hull and York. How can you hope to succeed as a burglar?"

16 A game warden in India has put up signs banning swimming in a crocodile-infested lake. "Swimming is prohibited. Survivors will be prosecuted." say the signs.

17 Returning to his car, a motorist found it badly damaged, and there was a note tucked behind his windscreen wiper. It read, "I have just run into your car. People are watching me write this. They think I am giving you my name and address. They are wrong!"

18 A man in Yugoslavia, Milivoja Ristic, has bought an old bus which he plans to eat over a period of two years. Mr Ristic has already eaten 22,500 razor blades, 127 kilos of glass, 3.6 kilos of lead shot, and a jeep. "I've always been like this," he said. "During the war, I ate ordinary food and it ruined my stomach."

19 "It's really exciting! I've never won anything like this before," a surprised Mrs White said yesterday afternoon. "My luck is changing!" The win provided Mrs White with the happiest moment since the death of her husband four weeks ago.

20 The inspector said that it was unlikely pollution was the cause. The fish bore no outward signs of disease. "These fish are perfectly healthy, except they are dead," he said.

21 Two guests and two waiters were treated for burns after a wedding cake exploded during a reception at Naples. "I think I must have used too much alcohol in the mix," the chef admitted.

22 When he was arrested while driving a 25-year-old Mini, Roberts admitted he had no insurance. "I broke my leg while trying to jack it up(,) and I had to get to the hospital," he explained.

Sergeant Adams said, "I heard the car from a mile away. At first I thought it was a bomb going off. I approached the car, which was going at about five miles an hour, and ordered the driver to stop. I found it had four completely bald tyres neither hand brake nor foot brake would work the steering was poor, there was no spare tyre(,) and it would engage only in first gear."

Mr Roberts explained that he had bought the car for £5. His wife thought they might sell it to a car museum.

23 A magician in Zambia assured a small crowd that if anyone gave him one pound he would be buried alive for two and a half hours. An on-looker gave him the money and helped to bury him. After waiting for the time to pass, the crowd dug him up. The magician was dead. His wife said, "Something must have gone wrong." A Zambian pound is worth 53 new pence.

24 An electrician from Belgrade broke the world record for staying underground. Accompanied by a pair of Canada ducks, he remained below for 463 days. During this period his wife divorced him.

25 Gardener Alex Wortley's home measures 1. metres by 0.9 metres by 1.4 metres. Alex, who is 73, lives in a wood and metal box. The box is in a back garden. Alex said yesterday, "Everyone has a right to their own place(,) and to me this is home. I am happy here. I have lived in boxes for more than thirty years. I have had this one for twenty years."

26 A piercing shriek cut through the silence of Worthing Magistrates Court yesterday. It was the sound of 36-year-old Paul Downs, who was imitating the noise of a fork-lift truck. Mr Downs was trying to demonstrate the type of noises that are keeping him awake at night.